November 6, 20

MW00875973

Wishing you wisdom in wealth!

Best Regards,

THE
GREAT

TAX

ESCAPE

**WHY MAKING MORE MONEY DOESN'T MEAN
YOU HAVE TO PAY MORE IN TAXES**

ERIC L. PIERRE, CPA

The Short Book Formula
PUBLISHING

"In America,
there are two tax systems:
one for the **informed**
and one for the **uninformed.**

Both are legal"

Judge Learned Hand

Eric L. Pierre
Copyright © 2024

Published by
The Short Book Formula Publishing

DISCLAIMER:

Table of Contents

Part 1 - Welcome

Who This Book Is For...01

My Promise To You..05

Introduction..11

Part 2 - The Great Tax Escape

Chapter 1: Why Smart Tax Planning is Good for Everyone.......19

Chapter 2: Why Your CPA May Be Letting You Down.............27

Chapter 3: Debunking Tax Myths: The Truth
About High-Income Tax Planning...................................39

Chapter 4: The Power of Vetted Tax Strategies..........................57

Chapter 5: Supercharging Your Retirement Accounts...............69

Chapter 6: Protecting Your Legacy with
Smart Estate Planning..79

Part 3 - The Path Forward

Chapter 7: Your Next Steps Toward Financial Freedom...........91

Resources and Social Media...97

About the Author...99

Praise For the Author

"Eric Pierre is not just a CPA; he's a financial strategist extraordinaire. His unique approach to tax strategies, akin to a champion fencer's precision, has saved me significant money and kept my business on the offensive. Eric's agility in navigating financial complexities, like that of a skilled lacrosse midfielder, has always led to significant savings and opportunities.

Off the financial court, Eric's integrity and professionalism are as consistent and reliable as a top-ranked tennis player's serve. His character is unshakeable, providing a solid foundation for our professional relationship.

As a real estate developer and founder of Firmspace, I've witnessed Eric parry potential financial risks with the skill of a master swordsman and ace tax savings like a grand slam champion. He's helped me significantly lower my taxes, allowing my projects and business to flourish.

Whether you're looking to defend against tax burdens or go on the offensive for financial growth, Eric Pierre is the expert you want in your corner. With Eric as your CPA, you're not just prepared; you're set to claim victory in finance and taxation. I, Justin Bayne, can confidently say this from my own experience."

Justin Bayne
President of Bayne Commercial

***

"I hired Eric Pierre back in the Summer of 2022. During this time, I've learned that Eric is more than just an accountant; he's a tax professional who listens and cares. He's worked with me as a client to curate a specific plan to help me make the most of my financial situation. He educates me through my blind spots and lists pros and cons of various approaches in an ever-changing tax landscape. Beyond that - I've come to know Eric personally and trust him as a friend.

If you're deciding how to move your finances from the red zone to the end zone, consider Eric Pierre."

Scott Hanson
TV Sportscaster

PART 1
WELCOME

Who This Book Is For

If you're holding this book, chances are, you're not just dreaming about success—you're living it! You're that entrepreneur who built an empire from the ground up, the exec calling shots in a Fortune 500 company, or the pro who's climbed to the top of your game. You've been breaking molds, shattering glass ceilings, and redefining what success looks like in your industry. You should be feeling on top of the world. Financially invincible, even. But something's not quite right yet, is it?

I feel you.

Every year, you watch a fat chunk of your hard-earned cash vanish into the IRS's coffers faster than a LeBron James slam dunk. It's like you're working half the year just to feed this tax beast that never seems to get full. Your CPA is giving you advice that's about as exciting as vanilla ice cream—all basic deductions and credits. You're nodding along, but deep down, you know there's got to be more to this story.

You've heard whispers about some next-level tax planning strategies. Complex trusts. Business restructuring. Offshore accounts. But it all sounds more complicated than the NBA's salary cap rules, and the last thing you want is to end up on the wrong side of the IRS. So you stick with what you know, all while that nagging feeling persists: you're leaving money on the table. And we're not talking about spare change here—we're talking serious money.

If this hits home, you're in the right place. This book is for high-flyers like you who are:

- Pulling in $500,000 or more annually (congrats, by the way!)

- Ready to take control of your tax game

- Tired of watching potential wealth slip through your fingers like a greased football

- Looking to play offense, not just defense, when it comes to taxes

- Hungry to learn strategies that could save you hundreds of thousands, even millions, over your lifetime

Now, let me be clear: this isn't about finding loopholes or some "one weird trick" to outsmart the IRS. If that's what you're after, I'm afraid you've picked up the wrong book, my friend. What you'll find here is a guide to smart, ethical tax planning that stands up to the most rigorous scrutiny. We're talking strategies used by the ultra-wealthy, adapted for the merely very successful—like you.

So, if you're:

- Ready to stop overpaying taxes and start building generational wealth

- Willing to put in the time and brain power to understand these concepts (trust me, it's worth it)

- Eager to work with a trusted advisor who speaks your language (and might throw in a sports metaphor or two)

Then it's time to turn the page. Because the truth about taxes that nobody's telling you? The secret playbook used by the ultra-wealthy to build empires? It's all in here. And it's about to change everything.

My Promise To You

Do you remember the first time you got a big paycheck? Let that memory hit you for a second. Picture yourself opening that envelope or logging into your bank account. Your heart's pounding like it's trying to break out of your chest, and you can't hold a wide grin. All those long hours, those sleepless nights, those sacrifices? They're finally paying off! You start mentally spending that money faster than Usain Bolt on race day - maybe it's a down payment on that dream house, a vacation that'd make your Instagram followers green with envy, or finally kicking those stubborn debts to the curb.

But then reality hits. Your eyes scan down to the bottom line, and suddenly, your stomach drops faster than a roller coaster. Where did all that money go? Nearly half of your hard-earned cash has pulled a Houdini and vanished into thin air. It's like watching the world's cruelest magic show. Instead of pulling a rabbit out of a hat, this magician - let's call him Uncle Sam - is making your dreams disappear right along with your money.

That surge of excitement you felt just moments ago? Gone. Now, you're feeling a mix of confusion, frustration, and maybe even a little anger. And let's be real, it's not just about the money. It's seeing all your blood, sweat, and tears get discounted faster than last year's iPhone. That deflating moment sticks with you like gum on your favorite shoes, leaving you wondering if climbing that career ladder is even worth it. Not exactly the kind of magic you were hoping for, was it?

But here's the thing: listen up 'cause this is important: it doesn't have to be this way.

And that's my first promise to you. I'm gonna show you there's a better way to handle your taxes. A way that's 100% legal and ethical and can potentially save you hundreds of thousands, or even millions, over your lifetime. We're talking game-changing strategies here, folks.

The Credentials Behind the Strategies

I've been in the trenches of the financial world for nearly two decades. Got myself a Master of Professional Accountancy and graduated with honors with a Bachelor of Business Administration in Accountancy from

Stephen F. Austin State University. (Go Lumberjacks!) I've been a licensed CPA in Texas since 2006 and added California to my resume in 2017.

I'm following in the footsteps of my dad, who was a CPA in the Empire State. You could say managing money well is in my blood - I was probably balancing checkbooks while still in diapers!

My career path? It's taken me through the corridors of Fortune 500 companies like Deloitte & Touche and Abbott Laboratories. I'm talking about global business operations across more industries than you can shake a stick at. This corporate background? It's given me a unique perspective on the challenges faced by high-income earners and businesses in managing their tax burdens. I've seen it all, and I know what works.

No Miracles, Just Proven Strategies

Now, let's get one thing straight. I'm not here to promise you overnight miracles or one-size-fits-all solutions. If anyone tries to sell you that, run for the hills. What I am going to give you is a roadmap. Think of it like Google Maps for your finances, but instead of avoiding traffic, we're avoiding unnecessary taxes. Here's what else you'll get in the pages of this book:

1. **We're gonna debunk some common tax myths that might be costing you a fortune.** You know that annoying voice in your head that says, "If I

make more money, I'll just end up paying more in taxes anyway"? We're gonna silence that voice once and for all.

2. **I'll give you access to the same advanced strategies used by the ultra-wealthy.** You don't need to be Jeff Bezos or Elon Musk to benefit from sophisticated tax planning. I'll show you how to leverage many of the same techniques used by the top 0.1%. It's time to level up your tax game!

3. **We're gonna dive deep into the tax code.** Now, I know it can be mind-numbingly boring. But I promise to break it down in a way that's not just understandable, but actually interesting. The tax code is like my sneaker collection - complex and always changing, but if you know what you're doing, you can make it work for you.

4. **I'll show you how to supercharge your retirement accounts.** We're talking strategies that could potentially turn a $100,000 investment into millions, all growing tax-free. It's like finding the cheat codes for the game of retirement.

5. **We'll explore how to protect your wealth through smart estate planning.** Because let's face it, you can't take it with you, but you can make sure it goes where you want it to go. It's about leaving a legacy, not just a pile of cash.

Safe, Sound, and Successful: Navigating Tax Strategies

Throughout this book, I'll share real-world examples and case studies. These are actual strategies I've implemented with my clients. (Don't worry; I've changed the names to protect the privacy of these very happy and now wealthier individuals. No snitching here!)

Let me just reiterate something: I know some people get nervous whenever anyone starts talking about tax strategies. But you're in a safe space here. In this book, there's nothing about finding loopholes or gaming the system. Everything we'll discuss is 100% above board and has been thoroughly vetted by top tax attorneys and CPAs. We're not looking to pick a fight with the IRS. (Trust me, that's one opponent you don't want to step in the ring with.) Instead, we're gonna work within the system, using it to our advantage like a pro basketball player working the refs.

I also promise to keep it 100 with you. I'm not here to sugarcoat things or tell you what you want to hear. If a strategy is too risky or not right for your situation, I'll tell you straight up. My goal is to give you the unvarnished truth about taxes and wealth-building, even if it sometimes challenges what you think you know.

Introduction

I started out just like many of you might have - climbing that corporate ladder like it was going out of style. For 12 long years, I was grinding at big-name firms like Deloitte & Touche and Abbott Laboratories. I was doing all the "right" things - putting in 60-70 hour weeks (yeah, you read that right), taking on some tough projects.

But something just wasn't clicking.

Despite busting my behind for these Fortune 500 heavyweights and giving it 110%, I hit the ceiling harder than a rookie in the NBA. My highest salary in the corporate world? A whopping $94,000. Now, don't get me wrong - that's not chump change by any means. But I knew I was worth more than that. I was consistently getting lowballed compared to my peers at other companies, even though I was often outperforming them.

It was a wake-up call. I realized that if I was gonna grind this hard, I needed to do it my way. I wanted to really help people and make a difference in their lives. And you know what? When you bring that kind of value, the money follows. It's about serving first, then getting paid what you're worth. That's the sweet spot – where you can crush it for your clients and build your own success at the same time.

That's when I decided to take the leap. In 2015, I founded Pierre Accounting. Talk about a game-changer!

Now, let me keep it 100 with you - it wasn't an easy decision. Leaving the security of a corporate job, especially as a black man in an industry about as diverse as a vanilla ice cream factory, was scary as hell. According to an AICPA report, only 2% of all U.S. Certified Public Accountants (CPAs) are Black. And get this - Black accountants make up just 1% of partners in accounting firms, while 91% of accounting firm partners are white. Those aren't just stats - that's the reality I was facing. But I knew I had to do it. Not just for myself but for all the clients I knew I could help.

You see, during my time in corporate America, I'd seen firsthand how the big dogs manage their tax burden. I'd watched high-flying execs and successful business owners work with top-tier accountants to slash their tax bills. And I realized something crucial: most people, even many high rollers, don't have access to these kinds of strategies. It's like they're playing checkers while the ultra-wealthy are playing 3D chess.

I wanted to change that game. I wanted to take all that knowledge I'd soaked up in the corporate world and make it accessible to a wider range of successful individuals. Not just the Jeff Bezos and Elon Musks of the world, but also the rising stars, the entrepreneurs, the professionals who are doing well but could be doing so much better with the right tax moves.

As I built my practice, I dove headfirst into advanced tax planning. I pushed myself to stay on top of tax law and strategy like it was the latest Jordan release. And you know what? It paid off big time. Not just for me but for my clients, too. I started seeing results that had me doing double-takes. Clients who'd been overpaying on taxes for years suddenly found themselves keeping hundreds of thousands of dollars more each year. Entrepreneurs who thought they were stuck with tax bills bigger than Texas discovered strategies that slashed their burden like a samurai sword.

But here's the real talk - it's not just about the money. What really gets me out of bed in the morning is seeing the impact this has on people's lives. It's about watching clients go from feeling stressed and overwhelmed about taxes to feeling like they've got the cheat codes to the game of finance. It's about helping them build the kind of wealth that can change their families' futures for generations. That's the real MVP stuff right there.

Now, let's break down how I approach tax planning. I like to think of it as building a championship team. Each tax strategy is like a player on your financial dream team, each with its own strengths and role to play:

1. **Income Tax Reduction Strategies:** These are your scoring machines, directly reducing your tax bill.

2. **Retirement Planning:** This is your defensive specialist, protecting your wealth from future tax hits and ensuring long-term financial security.

3. **Estate Planning:** Think of this as your coach, crucial for guiding your overall financial game plan and securing your legacy.

4. **Business Structure Optimization:** This is your versatile player, adapting to your changing financial needs and helping maximize tax efficiency in various situations.

5. **Charitable Giving Strategies:** This is your team captain, not only helping others but also providing significant tax benefits to you.

Just like the Golden State Warriors need more than just Steph Curry to win championships, a solid tax strategy requires a diverse array of tools and techniques.

These strategies need to work together seamlessly, each complementing the others to create a winning combination.

As we move forward in this book, remember this: my tax strategies are like a tailored Tom James suit - they fit perfectly and make you look good. Whether your income comes from a steady executive salary, the rollercoaster world of entrepreneurship, or the bright lights of entertainment or sports, we're going to craft a tax strategy that fits you well. It'll not only save you money but have you strutting into your accountant's office feeling like a million bucks (and keeping more of those bucks in your pocket, too).

Remember, it's not about how much you make - it's about how much you keep. And with the right strategies, you can keep a lot more, no matter what field you're balling in.

And who knows? Maybe one day, armed with the financial strategies we'll discuss in this book, you'll be joining me courtside, living out my dream of owning an NBA team. After all, in both sports and finance, anything is possible with the right game plan.

PART 2

THE
GREAT TAX
ESCAPE

Chapter 1

Why Smart Tax Planning is Good for Everyone

W e're about to flip the script on everything you thought you knew about taxes, wealth, and being a stand-up member of society. Let's talk about why paying less in taxes might actually make you a better citizen. I know, I know, it sounds crazy, right? But stick with me here.

In this chapter, we're gonna challenge some of those deep-seated beliefs you've got about money and taxes. How can smart tax planning line up with your personal values? How can it juice up the economy? And here's the kicker - how can it supercharge your ability to support the causes you care about? Buckle up because we're about to dive into all of that. But first, let's see where your head's at when it comes to taxes.

Alright, folks, it's time for a quick gut check. Rate these statements from 1 (hard disagree) to 5 (couldn't agree more):

1. Paying more in taxes makes me a better citizen.

2. I feel guilty when I think about reducing my tax bill.

3. Advanced tax strategies are only for the ultra-wealthy.

4. I'm afraid that trying to reduce my taxes might trigger an audit.

5. My current tax situation is the best I can hope for.

If you're scoring high on these, don't sweat it. You're in good company. A lot of my clients started out feeling the same way. But by the time we're done here, I'm betting you'll see things in a whole new light.

The Guilt Trap

Let me tell you about Mark. This guy built a business from scratch, hit it big, and then came to me feeling guilty about his success. Can you believe that?

"Maybe I should just pay whatever they say I owe," he told me, sounding like he'd just been caught with his hand in the cookie jar. "I don't want to be one of those rich guys who doesn't pay their fair share."

I hear this kind of thing all the time. It's like we've been programmed to think that minimizing taxes is greedy or irresponsible. But let me tell you, that view isn't just wrong - it's potentially harmful to you, your family, and believe it or not, to society as a whole.

The Truth About "Paying Your Fair Share"

Look, here's the deal: in 2018, the top 1% paid more taxes than the bottom 90% combined. That's not me talking - that's cold, hard facts. And get this - the top 50% of taxpayers? They shouldered 97% of all individual income taxes. So when people start yapping about the wealthy paying their "fair share," they often don't realize just how much high-earners are already ponying up.

But here's the real kicker - legally minimizing your taxes isn't about shirking your duty. It's about being a good steward of your resources. And here's the plot twist - it can actually help you do more good in the world.

The Multiplier Effect of Proper Tax Planning

Let's break this down with a simple example. Imagine you've got $100,000. You can either:

A) Pay it in taxes

B) Keep it through legal tax planning strategies

With Scenario A, that money goes to the government and gets spent according to the federal budget. You've got zero say in how it's used.

But with Scenario B? Now we're talking. You've got options:

- Reinvest in your business, potentially creating jobs and driving economic growth
- Donate to charities you care about, making a direct impact
- Invest in your local community through projects you believe in
- Fund your kids' education, breaking cycles of debt and creating opportunities
- Invest in innovative startups, fueling technological progress and job creation

In Scenario B, you're not just keeping more money. You're gaining the power to allocate resources in ways that align with your values and potentially create more value for society. Think of your money like a star player. You want it on the field, making plays, not sitting on the bench, right?

The Ethical Case for Tax Planning

Now, let's tackle the elephant in the room - and no, I'm not talking about that statue your Aunt Mildred gave you last Christmas. Is it ethical to actively try to reduce your taxes? I'd argue it's not just ethical - it's a moral imperative. Here's why:

Following the Law is Ethical: These tax strategies are 100% legal. They're not loopholes - they're intentional provisions in the tax code designed to incentivize certain behaviors and economic activities.

Resource Allocation: You, as an individual, are likely to be more efficient and targeted in allocating resources than the government. Why? Because you know your community, your industry, and the causes you care about intimately.

Economic Stimulus: Many tax minimization strategies involve activities that stimulate the economy - like investing in businesses or real estate. This creates jobs and drives growth.

Philanthropy: With more resources at your disposal, you have more capacity for charitable giving. Many of my clients who have implemented aggressive (but legal) tax planning strategies end up donating far more to charity than they saved in taxes.

Innovation Funding: Private capital, freed up through tax planning, often funds innovative startups and technologies that can solve major societal problems.

Real-World Impact: Taxes Saved, Communities Gained

Let me hit you with a real example. I've got this client, a tech entrepreneur we'll call Sarah. She used to shell out about $2 million in taxes every year. Through some strategic planning, we legally cut her tax bill by about $800,000 annually.

Now, here's where it gets good. Sarah didn't just save money - she turned into a one-woman community development machine! Check out what she did with that $800,000:

1. $300,000 went to funding a coding boot camp in an underserved community, creating tech opportunities for underprivileged youth.

2. $200,000 was invested in a green energy startup working on breakthrough solar technology.

3. $200,000 went to her alma mater to fund scholarships for first-generation college students.

4. The remaining $100,000 was used to start a mentorship program for women in tech.

The impact of these initiatives far outweighed what that $800,000 would have accomplished as part of the general tax fund. Sarah created direct, measurable change in areas she was passionate about. She felt like she'd won the lottery, but instead of blowing it on bling, she decided to change lives. That's what I call a touchdown for the community!

Reframing the Narrative

As Jay-Z said, "I'm not a businessman, I'm a business, man." That's how you need to think about your taxes.

It's not about dodging responsibility - it's about smart business.

It's time we change the narrative around wealth and taxes. Paying more in taxes than you legally owe doesn't make you a better citizen. Being a good citizen means:

- Following the law

- Contributing to economic growth

- Creating opportunities for others

- Supporting causes you believe in

- Investing in innovation and progress

All of these can be achieved - often more effectively - through smart tax planning rather than overpaying taxes.

Eric's Pro Tip:
"Remember, paying less in taxes isn't just about keeping more money - it's about what you do with that money."

Bringing It All Together

So, what's it gonna be? Are you ready to step up and take control of your tax game? Trust me, your wallet -

and your community - will thank you.

As we move forward in this book, exploring various tax strategies, I want you to think not just about the money you'll save, but about what you can do with that money. How can you use these resources to make a positive impact on your family, your community, and the world at large?

Remember, it's not about paying less. It's about consciously choosing where your money goes and what it does. That's not just smart financial planning - it's responsible citizenship.

Up next, we're gonna tackle a crucial question: Is your CPA really your financial MVP, or is it time to make some trades? We'll explore if your financial quarterback is fumbling the ball or if your starting pitcher is throwing nothing but wild pitches. Maybe it's time to go to the bullpen and bring in a fresh arm.

Or let's put it this way - is your CPA promising you a beautiful engagement ring but keeps making excuses about why it's not the right time? We'll dive into the signs that your current CPA might be letting you down and what to look for in a tax pro who can truly help you maximize your wealth and impact. You'll learn why many CPAs, despite their best intentions, may not be equipped to handle the complex tax situations of high-income earners like yourself. It's time to see if you need to upgrade your financial team to championship caliber.

Chapter 2

Why Your CPA
May Be Letting You Down

It's 2009, and the California sun's doing its best impression of a disco ball over La Jolla beach. Folks are packing up their coolers and shaking sand out of places they didn't even know they had, probably gearing up for a wild Saturday night in San Diego. My buddy and I were standing there, toes in the sand, gathering our stuff and shooting the breeze about life and our careers.

Now, at this point, I'm supposed to be living the dream. I'm the Michael Jordan of corporate accounting (minus the ten scoring titles and the championship rings). On paper, I'm balling. But in my gut? I've got this nagging feeling I'm letting my clients down harder than a bad stock tip.

My buddy must've picked up on my vibe 'cause just as we're about to bounce, he hits me with this:

"Eric, are you actually happy with this career path? You're out here making everyone else rich, but what about you, man?"

BAM! That question hit me like I'd just been tackled by the entire defensive line of the NFL. It was like someone finally turned up the volume on that little voice in my head. You know how it is - sometimes it takes a friend calling you out to really see what's what.

Right then and there, I knew I had to step up my game. My clients deserved a financial MVP, someone who could turn the tax code from a wealth-eating monster into a money-making machine. And let's be real - I deserved better too. I wanted that feeling of knowing I was out there making a real difference, not just pushing papers.

I was still stuck in the corporate game until 2015. For six long years, I saw firsthand why so many CPAs might be letting their clients down. The red tape, the cookie-cutter approaches, the focus on playing it safe instead of playing it smart - it was like trying to win the Super Bowl with one hand tied behind your back.

I realized that to really serve my clients, to give them the MVP treatment they deserved, I needed to break free from those corporate shackles. It wasn't an overnight change, but that sunset chat? It lit a fire under me that kept burning until I could finally make my move and do things my way.

Little did I know at the time that this beach conversation would set me on a path to revolutionize how I approached taxes and wealth-building for my clients.

The $425K Turning Point

Let me tell you about Harvey. This dude was a hotshot surgeon, pulling in $1 million a year. When he came to me for tax help, I did what any good corporate CPA would do – dotted all the i's, crossed all the t's, and handed him a tax bill for $425,528.

Harvey looked at that number and turned his head to me to say: "Eric, I spend more time at the hospital than I do with my kids, and this is the best you can do?"

The rest of his story you'll see in chapter 4. For now, I just wanna let you know that this moment hit me like a freight train. It was like that conversation with my buddy on the beach all over again, but this time in HD. Everything I'd been feeling, everything I knew I needed to change – it all came rushing back. This wasn't just about me anymore; it was about all the Harveys out there getting the short end of the stick.

Right then and there, I doubled down on my commitment. My clients needed more than just a number-cruncher. They deserved someone who'd turn the tax code into their personal ATM, not a black hole for their hard-earned cash. And I was gonna be that guy.

The CPA Comfort Trap: Why Even Good Accountants Fall Short

Now, don't get me wrong. Most CPAs out there are hardworking folks who genuinely want to help. But there are a bunch of reasons why they're not giving you the tax-saving strategies you really need. Let's break down this "CPA Comfort Trap":

- **Overwhelmed by Compliance Work:** Most CPAs are drowning in paperwork. They're so busy filling out last year's forms that they don't have time to think about next year's strategy. It's like trying to win a race by staring in the rearview mirror.

- **Lack of Specialized Knowledge:** Let me hit you with a fact: the tax code is over a million words long. That's more than the entire Harry Potter series! And it's constantly changing. For the average CPA, keeping up with all this while running a practice is like trying to drink from a fire hose.

- **Risk Aversion:** Most CPAs are like ostriches with their heads in the sand when it comes to advanced tax strategies. They're so scared of pushing the envelope that they stick to "safe" strategies, even when more aggressive (but still totally legal) options are available.

• **Misaligned Incentives:** Here's an uncomfortable truth: many CPAs actually benefit from you paying higher taxes. If they charge by the hour or based on how complicated your return is, they've got no reason to make things simpler or cheaper for you. That's why I'm all about flat-fee planning – it puts us on the same team.

• **One-Size-Fits-All Approach:** Every high-income earner's situation is unique. But many CPAs try to use the same basic tricks for all their clients. It's like me, a 6'8" guy wearing size 15 shoes, shopping at the same store as my 5'10" buddy who wears size 10. The clothes that fit him would make me look like I'm ready for a flood!

• **Lack of a Multidisciplinary Approach:** Real tax planning isn't just about knowing tax law. It's about estate planning, business structuring, investment strategies, and more. Many CPAs just don't have the network or know-how to bring all these pieces together.

• **Focusing on the Wrong Metrics:** Too many CPAs judge their performance on whether they got you a refund this year. But that's short-term thinking. It's like celebrating winning a battle while losing the war.

• **Resentment of Wealthy Clients:** This might shock you, but there's a trend of CPAs who actually resent their high-income clients. They've bought into this idea that the wealthy don't pay their "fair share." Skeptical? Please take a look at these tweets from tax experts and finance influencers:

Francine Lipman
@Narfnampil

"Many of these subsidies disproportionately benefit the wealthy, worsen racial inequality, create generational inequities, and weaken states' fiscal positions without offering any meaningful upside." #TaxTwitter @iteptweets

Francine Lipman
@Narfnampil

The tax reporting disclosure requirement is to equalize the taxing field/most of us who are W2/earners report all our income & but the top 10% who are pass thru income earners are responsible for 70% of the $600 BILLION ANNUAL tax gap! It is about wealthy tax cheats! #TaxTwitter

Samantha Jacoby @jacsamoby · Sep 29, 2021

Two Wall Street/bank veterans take on bank lobbyists' attempts to quash Biden's information reporting proposal, calling it a "critical component" of the plan to rebuild the IRS.
bloomberg.com/opinion/articl...

Brakeyshia R. Samms (she/her)
@BrakeyshiaSamms

This #TaxDay, Congress should make the wealthy and corporations pay their fair share of taxes so we can make crucial investments in working families, not cut services benefiting working families! #TaxTwitter

4:42 PM · Apr 18, 2023 · **1,611** Views

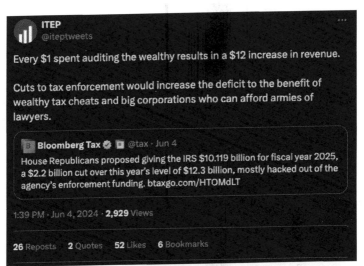

ITEP
@iteptweets

Every $1 spent auditing the wealthy results in a $12 increase in revenue.

Cuts to tax enforcement would increase the deficit to the benefit of wealthy tax cheats and big corporations who can afford armies of lawyers.

> **Bloomberg Tax** ✔ 🔲 @tax · Jun 4
> House Republicans proposed giving the IRS $10.119 billion for fiscal year 2025, a $2.2 billion cut over this year's level of $12.3 billion, mostly hacked out of the agency's enforcement funding. btaxgo.com/HTOMdLT

1:39 PM · Jun 4, 2024 · **2,929** Views

26 Reposts   **2** Quotes   **52** Likes   **6** Bookmarks

James Tate ✔
@JamesTate121

Kevin O'Leary said all rich people cheat on taxes in every City so why go after Donald Trump. The sense of entitlement with these billionaires is sickening. F that guy.

8:58 AM · Mar 26, 2024 · **864.1K** Views

2,681 Reposts   **356** Quotes   **11.5K** Likes   **53** Bookmarks

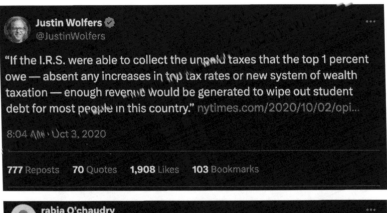

> **Justin Wolfers** ✓
> @JustinWolfers
>
> "If the I.R.S. were able to collect the unpaid taxes that the top 1 percent owe — absent any increases in top tax rates or new system of wealth taxation — enough revenue would be generated to wipe out student debt for most people in this country." nytimes.com/2020/10/02/opi...
>
> 8:04 AM · Oct 3, 2020
>
> **777** Reposts   **70** Quotes   **1,908** Likes   **103** Bookmarks

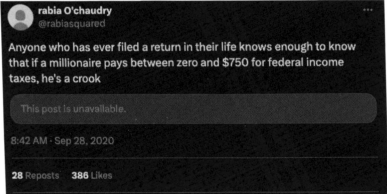

> **rabia O'chaudry**
> @rabiasquared
>
> Anyone who has ever filed a return in their life knows enough to know that if a millionaire pays between zero and $750 for federal income taxes, he's a crook
>
> This post is unavailable.
>
> 8:42 AM · Sep 28, 2020
>
> **28** Reposts   **386** Likes

The $500K+ Club: Unlocking the Bigger Playbook

Now, you might be thinking, "Eric, can't any CPA help me save on taxes?" Well, yes and no. Any decent CPA can help with basic deductions and credits. But when you're making $500,000 or more annually? That's when you unlock what I call "the bigger playbook."

Why $500,000? It's not just a random number. At this level, the game changes. You've got more strategies available, and they're more powerful. It's like upgrading from checkers to chess – suddenly, you've got a whole new set of moves.

Let me give you an example. I had a client, Mike, who came to me when he first hit that $500K mark. His old CPA was competent, but he was playing little league ball in a major league game.

When Mike's income hit $500K, we opened up a whole new world. We set up a defined benefit plan that let him stash away over $100K pre-tax annually. We restructured his real estate investments for better depreciation. We even set up a charitable trust that let him support his favorite causes while saving big on taxes.

The result? In year one, we slashed Mike's effective tax rate by 15 percentage points compared to his old CPA. That's over $75,000 in savings – and it compounds year after year.

That's the power of the bigger playbook. It's not just about paying less in taxes (though that's pretty sweet). It's about using the tax code to turbocharge your wealth-building, protect your assets, and crush your long-term financial goals.

So, what should you look for in a CPA who can play in the big leagues? Here's your scouting report:

1. Specializes in high-income tax strategies
2. Takes a proactive, forward-looking approach
3. Has a network of expert teammates in other fields
4. Has a track record of big tax savings for clients
5. Isn't afraid to be aggressive (while staying in bounds)
6. Uses a flat-fee model that puts them on your team
7. Never stops learning about new tax laws
8. Has experience facing off against the IRS and winning

Finding a CPA with all these qualities is like finding a unicorn in the wild. But they're out there. And when you find one (hint, hint), it can revolutionize your financial future.

Eric's Pro Tip:
"Don't just take my word for it. Always ask for the game tape – get explanations, see the relevant tax code sections, understand how each strategy works. A truly valuable tax strategy should hold up under replay review."

Bringing It All Together

As we wrap this up, take a moment to think about your relationship with taxes. For a lot of high-income earners, taxes are like that annoying rival team you just can't beat. But what if we could change the game?

Imagine viewing the tax code not as a burden, but as a playbook where the rewards for mastery are huge. It's not about finding loopholes or cheating the system – it's about knowing the rules inside and out and playing to win.

In the next chapter, we'll tackle one of the biggest myths in taxation – the idea that making more money always means paying more taxes. This belief has benched countless high achievers. But with the right strategies, you can break free from this mental block and enter a whole new league of financial success.

Chapter 3

Debunking Tax Myths: The Truth About High-Income Tax Planning

"Pay your taxes, y'all!"

That's what Jay-Z once rapped, and sure, it's solid advice... if you're cool with the IRS taking a bigger bite out of your wallet than Jaws at a beach party. But what if I told you there's a way to keep Uncle Sam happy and still have enough left over for that Cartier watch you've been eyeing, the family member you'd like to help, or the worthy cause you want to support?

Welcome to the big leagues of tax planning, where most CPAs are playing checkers while we're out here playing 3D chess. In this chapter, we're about to flip the script on some myths that have been holding you back from the tax game's god-tier strategies.

We're talking about misconceptions that are so persistent that they make flat-earth theories look reasonable. But don't worry - by the time we're done here, you'll be seeing through these fallacies like they're made of Saran Wrap. And the best part? Understanding this stuff could save you more money over your lifetime than the GDP of a small country.

So buckle up, because we're about to take your tax game from Honda Civic to Rolls-Royce Ghost. Once you're riding in style like this, you'll never want to go back to the tax planning slow lane.

The Big Money Tax Puzzle

Let's tackle the elephant in the room - the belief that, inevitably, making more money means paying more in taxes. I've seen this myth stick around like gum on your shoe, keeping countless high-achievers from reaching their full potential. It's like a self-imposed glass ceiling, and today, we're going to shatter it.

Back when I was cutting my teeth at Fortune 500 companies like Deloitte & Touche and Abbott Laboratories, I saw firsthand how the big players manage their tax burden. They don't just roll over and accept paying more taxes as they earn more. They apply strategies, and guess what? So can you.

Now, you might be thinking, "But Eric, aren't higher tax brackets a fact of life?" Well, yes and no. It's time to pull back the curtain on how taxes really work when you start playing in the financial big leagues.

Tax Brackets 101: What You Need to Know

Many folks think that when they move into a higher tax bracket, all their income gets taxed at that higher rate. But that's about as accurate as saying that the Las Vegas Raiders are going to win the Super Bowl next year. (p.s. I root for them anyway because I grew up in a Silver and Black household - they were the very first team my dad saw play when he immigrated from Haiti) Here's the real deal: The U.S. tax system is progressive, meaning we have different tax rates for different levels of income. As your income increases, you move into higher tax brackets. But here's the crucial part: only the income within each bracket gets taxed at that rate.

Think of it this way: your income doesn't suddenly jump to the highest tax rate when you make more money. It's not like you're suddenly in the tax big leagues just because you hit a financial home run. Instead, it's taxed in chunks, with each chunk corresponding to a different bracket.

Let's break it down with some numbers. Say you're a single filer making a cool million in 2021. You'd be in the 37% tax bracket, which sounds scarier than a horror movie marathon, right? But here's where people often get confused. Your effective federal income tax rate - that's the percentage you actually pay when all is said and done - would only be about 31.5%.

And that's before we've even started applying any advanced tax strategies! Can you believe it? Imagine what we could do with some smart planning. It's like finding extra gear in your sports car you didn't even know existed.

The Five Biggest Tax Myths for High Earners

Myth 1: Tax Planning is Too Complex for Me to Understand

Ever felt like tax planning is some kind of secret code that only CPAs can understand? You're not alone. Many people assume it's so complex that they should just leave it to the pros and hope for the best.

The Truth: While tax law can be more confusing than the plot of Inception, the principles of good tax planning are often surprisingly straightforward. Think of it like driving a car – you don't need to know how every part of the engine works to get from point A to point B safely.

A good tax strategist should be able to explain their recommendations in terms that don't make your head spin. You're the CEO of your financial life, after all. You wouldn't run a company without understanding the basics of your business strategy, would you?

Take a moment to reflect: Have you ever avoided

asking questions about your taxes because you thought you wouldn't understand the answer? How might your financial situation improve if you had a clearer grasp of your tax strategy? It's time to start asking those questions and taking control of your financial playbook.

Myth 2: Tax Planning is Only for the Ultra-Wealthy

If you're not sipping champagne on your private yacht, you might think advanced tax planning is out of your league. But let me tell you a secret – you don't need to be Jeff Bezos or Elon Musk to benefit from smart tax strategies.

The Truth: There's a whole toolbox of powerful techniques available for folks making high six or seven-figure incomes. In fact, tax planning often packs a bigger punch for people in this range than for the ultra-wealthy. It's like having a secret weapon in your financial arsenal.

Remember that real estate developer I mentioned who cut his taxes to zero? He was making just over a million, not billions. And that Silicon Valley exec who slashed her effective tax rate in half? Also in the seven-figure club. These aren't unicorns, folks - they're just smart players who know the rules of the game.

Myth 3: Aggressive Tax Planning Will Trigger an Audit

I get it. The thought of an IRS audit is about as appealing as a root canal without anesthesia. Many people are so paralyzed by this fear that they avoid any attempt to significantly reduce their taxes.

The Truth: Hold onto your W-2s, folks, because I'm about to drop a truth bomb that'll blow your mind. According to the IRS Data Book, the overall chance of being audited is a measly 0.2%. That's right, only 1 out of every 500 returns gets the audit treatment. It's like winning the lottery, except instead of a giant check, you get a date with Uncle Sam's accountants.

But here's the kicker - most audits are triggered by underreporting income from 1099s and the like. It's not your savvy tax planning that's likely to raise eyebrows; it's forgetting to report that side hustle income.

Now, I'm not saying we should play fast and loose with the rules. The strategies I advocate are all based on clear provisions of the tax code and relevant case law. They're designed to stand up to scrutiny like Muhammad Ali in his prime. If you do end up being that 1 in 500, we'll be ready to go toe-to-toe with the IRS and come out swinging.

And let me tell you, I'm not just talking the talk here. Back in 2019, the IRS decided to put my own returns under the microscope. Guess what? When the dust settled, there wasn't a single change to my income. That's right; I walked out of that audit as I would walk into Ashe Stadium, confident and ready to battle for the US Open Men's Championship Final, facing an opponent as formidable as Roger Federer - prepared and eager for the next challenge.

In fact - and here's where it gets more interesting than a plot twist in a tax law thriller - a lack of planning often poses a greater risk. When you're consistently overpaying your taxes, you're more likely to make mistakes or take inappropriate deductions out of desperation to lower your bill. It's like trying to fit into your old jeans by holding your breath - it might work for a moment, but it's not a long-term solution.

With proper planning, everything is documented and justified. It's like having a well-organized closet - if someone comes looking, you know exactly where everything is and why it's there.

Myth 4: Tax Planning is Unethical or Unpatriotic

Ever felt a twinge of guilt about trying to minimize your taxes? Like maybe you're not doing your civic duty? I've been there too. But let's unpack this like we're opening a beautiful bag from Louis Vuitton from that stunning box.

The Truth: There's nothing unethical or unpatriotic about legally minimizing your tax burden. In fact, the tax code is intentionally written with numerous incentives and opportunities for reducing taxes. By taking advantage of these, you're actually acting in accordance with the intent of the law.

As Judge Learned Hand once wrote, "Anyone may arrange his affairs so that his taxes shall be as low as possible; he is not bound to choose that pattern which best pays the Treasury. There is not even a patriotic duty to increase one's taxes." And let me tell you, that guy was dropping knowledge bombs like it was his job (which, I guess, it kind of was).

Think about it this way: By reducing your tax burden, you're freeing up capital that can be invested in growing businesses, creating jobs, and stimulating the economy. Often, this can have a more positive impact than if that money had gone to the government. You're not dodging your responsibilities - you're optimizing your impact.

Myth 5: Once I Find a Good Strategy, I'm Set for Life

Wouldn't it be nice if we could set up our tax strategy once and forget about it? Unfortunately, that's about as realistic as expecting your one trip to the gym last January to keep you fit forever.

The Truth: Tax planning is not a one-and-done deal, but an ongoing process. The tax code is always changing, and strategies that work well one year might fizzle out the next. Plus, your personal and financial situation will evolve over time, necessitating adjustments to your tax strategy.

This is why I'm a big fan of a proactive, year-round approach to tax planning. My high-net-worth clients typically have check-ins every six months to review their situation and make any necessary adjustments. It's like regular maintenance on your car – a little attention now can prevent big problems down the road.

Case Studies: The Power of Informed Tax Planning

Let's bring these concepts to life with a couple of real-world examples. These aren't just hypotheticals - these are real people who've used these strategies to level up their financial game.

James's Real Estate Revolution

James, a wildly successful real estate developer, came to me with a problem that might sound familiar. He'd amassed a net worth of $40 million before age 40 and was pulling in $2-7 million annually. Impressive, right? But despite working with one of the biggest, most prestigious accounting firms in the country, James consistently paid 33-40% in federal taxes alone. That's like winning the lottery and then having to give away half your ticket!

When James first heard about the work I'd done for his friend Troy, another high-net-worth individual, he was intrigued but skeptical. It seemed too good to be true that I'd helped Troy reduce his effective tax rate to between 0-10% over the past few years.

After a comprehensive review of James's past returns, I was shocked at what I found. The previous firm had missed more opportunities than a basketball team with no point guard. They had failed to properly classify James as a real estate professional, which alone cost him hundreds of thousands in deductions.

We immediately filed amended returns for the previous three years, resulting in a $200,000 refund for James. But that was just the warm-up. By implementing a carefully crafted set of powerful, IRS-approved tax strategies, we were able to reduce James's effective tax rate to between 14-15% on his multi-million dollar income going forward. This meant James was now keeping close to 85 cents of every dollar he earned, instead of losing almost half to taxes like he had been before. Now, that's what I call a game-changer!

Adam's Arbitrage Adventure

Now, let's look at a different scenario. Adam is a Wall Street wonder kid. By his late 30s, he was making the kind of money that turns heads even in the cutthroat world of finance - $5 million a year. But even Adam, with all his financial wizardry, was feeling the sting of a $400,000 tax bill.

When Adam came to me, he was more cautious than a bear in a bull market. "Eric," he said, "I've heard about strategies to minimize the tax burden, but I'm worried about attracting the wrong kind of attention from the IRS. What can we do that won't land me in hot water?"

I appreciated his caution. After all, in finance, one wrong move can put you in some very complicated situations. But I had an ace up my sleeve - a strategy involving an insurance policy that would allow him to defer his taxes for seven years.

His eyes lit up like a trader who just spotted an arbitrage opportunity. "If I'm understanding this correctly," he said, leaning forward, "we're essentially creating an arbitrage opportunity using the time value of money?"

"Exactly," I replied. "By deferring the $400,000 tax payment, you're free to invest that capital. Given the current inflation rate of 4.2%, that $400,000 will be equivalent to about $516,000 in 2026. You'll only need to repay the original $400,000, without interest or penalties."

Adam was intrigued, but like any good financial professional, he wanted to make sure we weren't coloring outside the lines.

I assured Adam that this strategy was as rock-solid as they come. Now, you might be wondering, 'Eric, how can you be so confident about this?' Well, let's just say I have access to some pretty powerful resources that allow me to vet these strategies thoroughly. But more on that in the next chapter - I promise it's a game-changer you won't want to miss.

What I can tell you now is that this strategy has been scrutinized by tax courts and is fully compliant with IRS regulations. When I recommend a strategy to my clients, you can bet it's been put through its paces more times than my favorite pair of Air Jordans.

Over the next few months, we put the plan into action. Adam, being the investment guru he is, made the most of the deferred tax amount, turning it into a significant profit.

The Truth About Making More and Keeping More

These case studies illustrate a crucial point: strategic tax planning isn't about pinching pennies. For high earners, we're talking about hundreds of thousands, even millions of dollars over time. It's the difference between good wealth building and generational wealth creation.

Let's crunch some numbers to really drive this home. Remember Adam, our Wall Street trader? Here's how the numbers broke down:

That's over $700,000 in additional wealth created just from one strategy. And remember, this is on top of other tax-saving measures we implemented. It's like finding a vintage pair of sneakers at a garage sale - unexpected and incredibly valuable.

Now, here's where it gets really exciting. Let's say Adam invests his tax savings every year for 20 years, assuming a 7% annual return:

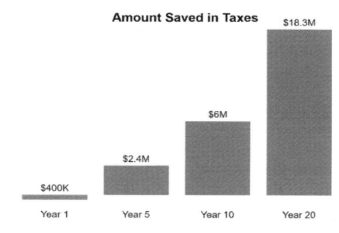

Amount Saved in Taxes

Scenario	Before Strategic Planning	After Strategic Planning
Gross Income	$5,000,000	$5,000,000
Federal Tax	$1,850,000	N/A
Effective Federal Tax Rate	37%	N/A
Tax Deferred	N/A	$400,000
Immediate Tax Savings	N/A	$400,000
Potential Investment Growth (7% annual return over 7 years)	N/A	$319,200
Total Benefit	N/A	$719,200

That's right - over 20 years, those annual tax savings could grow to over $18 million! And remember, this is just from the tax savings alone, not including his regular investments. It's like compound interest on steroids!

Overcoming Tax Mitigation Trauma

When we talk about taxes, we often focus on the numbers - the dollars and cents that leave our bank accounts each year. But there's another cost that's rarely discussed: the emotional toll of taxes. As someone who's worked with countless high-income earners, I've seen firsthand how taxes can create stress, anxiety, and even a condition I call "tax mitigation trauma."

Tax mitigation trauma is a psychological state that develops when individuals have had negative experiences with tax planning in the past. It's like being afraid to get back on a bike after a nasty fall. It often manifests as:

- Extreme risk aversion to any tax strategy beyond basic deductions

- Anxiety about IRS audits, even when following the law meticulously

- Guilt or shame about wanting to minimize tax burden

- Paralysis when it comes to making financial decisions due to tax implications

If you've experienced any of these feelings, know that

you're not alone. Many of my clients come to me with some degree of tax mitigation trauma. But here's the good news: with the right approach and guidance, you can overcome this and take control of your tax situation. It's like physical therapy for your financial mindset.

Action Steps: Assessing Your Current Tax Situation

As we wrap up this chapter, I want you to take a moment to reflect on your own tax approach. Here's a quick checklist to help you evaluate where you stand:

1. Do you know your effective tax rate for the past year?

2. Have you explored tax strategies beyond basic deductions and credits?

3. Are you comfortable asking questions about your tax situation?

4. Do you view tax planning as an ongoing process or a once-a-year event?

5. Have you considered how your tax strategy aligns with your long-term financial goals?

If you answered "no" to any of these questions, don't worry. You're exactly where you need to be to start making positive changes. It's like being at the starting line of a race - you're in the perfect position to begin your journey.

Eric's Pro Tip:
"I once had a client who was scared to make more money because he thought it would all go to taxes. After we implemented some smart strategies, he actually kept a higher percentage of his income as he earned more. Don't let tax myths hold you back from reaching your full earning potential! It's like refusing to run faster because you think you'll use up all your energy - sometimes, you've got to push yourself to see what you're really capable of."

Bringing It All Together

We've covered a lot of ground in this chapter, from debunking common myths to exploring real-world case studies of effective tax planning. The key takeaway is this: with the right knowledge and strategies, you can significantly reduce your tax burden while building lasting wealth.

Remember, every dollar you save in taxes is a dollar you can invest in growing your wealth, supporting your family, contributing to causes you care about, or simply enjoying the fruits of your labor. It's like finding money in your couch cushions, except instead of spare change, we're talking about potentially millions of dollars.

As we move forward, I challenge you to view taxes not as an unavoidable burden, but as an area of opportunity. Each myth you overcome and each strategy you implement brings you one step closer to financial empowerment. You've worked hard for your money; now, let's make sure you keep more of it.

In the next chapter, we'll dive deeper into the power of vetted tax strategies, exploring how you can leverage sophisticated techniques to take your wealth-building to the next level.

Chapter 4

The Power of Vetted Strategies

Chris Rock once said, "If poor people knew how rich rich people are, there would be riots in the streets." Now, I'm not here to start a riot, but I am about to let you in on a little secret of the wealthy: it's not just about how much you make but how much you keep.

What if I told you we could cut your tax bill in half and make you feel like a hero in the process? Sounds too good to be true? Well, as Chris Rock might say, "Good thing I'm about to blow your mind!" Just don't tell my momma I'm out here causing trouble with the tax code.

In this chapter, we're gonna pull back the curtain on the powerful, vetted tax strategies that the ultra-wealthy use to keep more of their hard-earned money. Whether you're a high-flying surgeon, a Wall Street prodigy, or somewhere in between, you're about to discover how to turn your tax bill from a burden into a wealth-building opportunity. Get ready to join the ranks of the financially savvy - no rioting necessary.

The Redeem Team: Your Access to Elite Tax Strategies

I know what you're thinking: "Eric, these strategies sound great, but how can I be sure they're legit and up-to-date?" This is where my Redeem Team comes in - a powerful resource that sets my approach apart from your average CPA.

Think of it as when USA Basketball brought in a super team in 2008 to bring back the gold in basketball. This is us helping clients redeem themselves from overpaying taxes with our own version of Kobe Bryant and LeBron James. Think of me as the Kobe Bryant of tax strategies - I'm here to lead the team and make game-winning plays for your finances.

My "Redeem Team" is an exclusive network of the top 1% of tax professionals in the country. We're talking about over 400 elite CPAs, tax attorneys, and financial experts who are at the cutting edge of tax strategy. But it's not just about having smart people in a room. The Redeem Team is a network where we have a rigorous system for vetting, testing, and perfecting tax strategies before they ever reach my clients.

Here's how it works:

1. **Strategy Identification:** We're always on the hunt for new tax-saving strategies. These might come from new interpretations of tax law, recent court cases, or innovative applications of existing rules.

2. **Rigorous Analysis:** Once we spot a potential strategy, we put it through the wringer. Our team of experts dissects every aspect, examining it from legal, financial, and practical perspectives.

3. **Real-World Testing:** We don't just theorize. We test these strategies in real-world scenarios to make sure they work as intended.

4. **Legal Validation:** Our network includes top tax attorneys who review each strategy to ensure it complies with current tax law. We even examine IRS private letter rulings and audit records to gauge how the IRS views similar strategies.

5. **Ongoing Monitoring:** The tax landscape is always changing, like the latest technology trends. We stay on top of legal and regulatory changes that might affect our strategies, allowing us to adapt quickly.

6. **Peer Review:** Before a strategy gets the green light, it's peer-reviewed by multiple Redeem Team members. This extra layer of scrutiny helps catch any potential issues and refines the strategy further.

Let me break it down for you. When you work with me, you're not just getting one CPA's opinion. You're tapping into a brain trust of the nation's top tax minds. Every strategy I recommend has been vetted, tested, and proven effective by this elite network.

Let me give you an example. Remember Adam, our Wall Street trader? The insurance strategy we used to defer his taxes wasn't something I cooked up overnight. It was a strategy that had been thoroughly vetted by the Redeem Team. We examined case studies of its successful use, analyzed relevant tax court rulings, and even had it reviewed by former IRS officials within our network. By the time I recommended it to Adam, I was confident it would stand up to any scrutiny.

This level of due diligence is something most CPAs simply can't offer. They might read about a strategy in a journal or hear about it at a conference, but they don't have the resources to thoroughly vet and test it before recommending it to clients. With the Redeem Team, we're not just reading about cutting-edge strategies - we're creating them.

The power of the Redeem Team extends beyond just vetting strategies. As a member, I have on-demand access to some of the brightest minds in tax planning. If I encounter a unique situation or complex problem, I can tap into this network for insights and solutions. It's like having a team of world-class specialists on speed dial, ready to help craft the perfect solution for your specific needs.

But what does this mean in the real world? How does this network of expertise translate into tangible benefits for high-earners like you? Let me introduce you to Harvey, a client whose story perfectly illustrates the power of these vetted strategies in action.

Harvey's Headache: The Return

Remember Harvey, the hotshot surgeon I introduced you to back in Chapter 2? Well, his story didn't end there – and neither did my journey to becoming the tax-slaying CPA I am today.

When we first met, Harvey was pulling in $1 million a year, and I managed to trim his tax bill from $425,528 to something more palatable. But I'll be honest with you – back then, I was still learning the ropes of advanced tax strategy. I helped Harvey, sure, but I knew I could do better.

Fast forward a few years, Harvey's career had gone supernova, pushing the boundaries of medical science and giving patients second chances at life. By his mid-40s, he was raking in $10 million annually, split between his work at a prestigious hospital and his thriving private practice.

But with great success came an even greater headache. Harvey called me one day, looking more stressed than a rapper facing an IRS audit.

"Eric," he said, collapsing into the chair across from me, "remember when you helped me before? Well, I need you now more than ever. I just went over the numbers with my accountant. My tax bill this year is $4.4 million. Do you think you can help me again?"

I couldn't help but smile. This time, I was ready. More than ready. "Harvey," I said, "let me ask you something. What if I told you we could cut that tax bill in half and make you feel like a hero at the same time?"

"I'm listening," he said.

Over the next few hours, we crafted a plan that would make both Harvey's and his accountant's heads spin. We set up a donor-advised fund focused on supporting research into innovative neurological treatments. This wasn't just about saving taxes - it was about creating a legacy.

Fast forward another year, and Harvey's donor-advised fund was funding cutting-edge research projects at medical institutions across the country. His tax bill? Slashed to $2 million. That's $2.4 million back in his pocket.

The best part wasn't even about the money. Harvey was now changing lives and funding investments in what he believed in. He was making a difference inside and outside of the operating room. That's what I call a slam dunk in both tax savings and life impact.

Choosing Your Path: Mitigation or Deferral?

Now, let's talk about choosing the right strategy for you. In the tax world, it all boils down to two main approaches: mitigation (like Harvey's charitable strategy) and deferral.

Choosing between mitigation and deferral can be tough - they're both top-tier choices, but the right pick depends on your needs and financial game plan. Here are a few questions to consider:

1. What are your financial goals for the next 5, 10, or 20 years?

2. How much risk are you comfortable with in your tax planning?

3. Are there causes or investments you're passionate about that could align with tax mitigation strategies?

4. Do you have the financial stability and expertise to benefit from tax deferral strategies?

Your answers to these questions will help guide you toward the tax optimization approach that fits you like a custom-tailored suit.

The Tax-Saving Toolbox

Now, let's talk specifics. Here are some strategies you might want to consider:

1. **Strategic Use of Business Entities:** This is about choosing the right tool for the job. An S-Corporation, for instance, can help reduce self-employment taxes.

2. **Real Estate Investment Strategies:** Real estate offers benefits like depreciation, 1031 exchanges, and potential "real estate professional" status. It's versatile and always in style.

3. **Retirement Account Optimization:** This goes way beyond maxing out your 401(k). We're talking backdoor Roth IRAs, mega backdoor Roths, and cash balance plans. These are like the limited-edition sneakers of the tax world - not everyone knows about them, but they can be game-changers. (Don't worry, we'll dive deeper into these in the next chapter.)

4. **Charitable Giving Strategies:** Remember Harvey? There are sophisticated approaches to charitable giving that can significantly reduce your tax burden while supporting causes you care about.

5. Timing Strategies: In tax planning, timing isn't everything - but it's pretty darn close. The when can be just as important as the how much.

Let me break this down using something I know inside and out - my footwear collection. Yeah, I've got a wall of sneakers that would make a Nike store jealous, but don't think for a second that's all I'm packing.

Tax strategies are like my shoe game - diverse and purpose-driven. Sometimes, you need those Air Jordans for agility and other times; you've got to pull out the Ferragamos to make a statement.

Here's the deal: Just like you wouldn't rock Yeezys to a black-tie event or Italian leather to a pickup game, not every tax strategy fits every financial situation. It's about knowing when to lace up the sneakers and when to slip on the loafers.

In the tax world, I'm not just throwing strategies at the wall to see what sticks. I'm carefully selecting the right moves for your specific situation. Whether we need to be quick and agile with creative deductions or smooth and sophisticated with long-term planning, I've got the strategy to match.

Eric's Pro Tip:

"Think of tax strategies like my sneaker collection - each one has its purpose and value. Just as I carefully curate my collection, I meticulously vet each tax strategy. One of my clients, a neurosurgeon, cut his tax bill in half using a carefully selected combination of strategies. It's all about finding the right fit for your financial situation."

Bringing It All Together

Every dollar saved in taxes is a dollar you can invest to grow your wealth, support your family, or contribute to causes you care about. It's like finding money in your couch cushions, except instead of loose change, we're talking about potentially millions of dollars.

So, ask yourself: What could you do with an extra million dollars? Expand your business? Fund your children's education? Support a cause you're passionate about. The possibilities are endless.

As we wrap up this chapter, I want you to do something for me. Imagine your life with a significantly reduced tax burden. How would it change your financial picture, your stress levels, and your ability to achieve your dreams?

Hold onto that vision. Because with the strategies we've discussed and the ones we're about to explore, it might be closer to reality than you think. We're not just talking about saving a few bucks here and there - we're talking about transforming your financial future.

I'm not just here to save you money - I'm here to help you build the life you've been dreaming of. Think of me as your financial point guard, ready to assist you in scoring big against the IRS.

In the next chapter, we'll dive deep into the world of retirement account strategies. We'll explore how these powerful tools can turbocharge your wealth-building efforts and potentially shave years off your working life.

Chapter 5

Supercharging Your Retirement Accounts

We're about to dive into something that most folks get all wrong. Retirement accounts aren't just piggy banks you toss a few coins into and hope for the best. Nah, these babies can be turbocharged wealth-building machines for high-rollers like you.

You see, the real magic of retirement accounts isn't in their basic function. It's in how you can strategically leverage them to build an empire. When you play this game right, these accounts become more than just savings vessels – they're tax-efficient wealth accelerators that can dramatically alter your financial trajectory.

In this chapter, we're gonna break down some advanced techniques that'll have your retirement accounts working overtime. We're not just talking about

Eric L. Pierre

maxing out your 401(k) here. We're talking sophisticated methods that could potentially save you millions in taxes over your lifetime while setting you up for explosive, tax-free growth.

Maximizing Contributions: Beyond the Basics

First things first, let's talk about filling up that retirement tank. For 2021, here's how much you can legally stuff into different types of retirement accounts:

Account Type	Annual Contribution Limit	Limit for Age 50+
Work-sponsored 401(k)	$19,500	$26,000
Individual Retirement Account (IRA)	$6,000	$7,000
Solo 401(k) (self-employed)	$58,000	$64,500

But what if you're a high earner and want to save even more? Don't worry; I've got some tricks up my sleeve. Let me break down three game-changers for you:

1. The "Backdoor" Roth IRA

Imagine there's an exclusive club (Roth IRA) that doesn't allow high earners to join directly. The "backdoor" method is like finding a secret entrance. Here's how it works:

- First, you put money into a traditional IRA. Anyone can do this, regardless of income.

- Then, you convert that traditional IRA into a Roth IRA.

- You'll need to pay some taxes when you do this conversion, but after that, your money grows tax-free, and you won't pay taxes when you take it out in retirement.

2. The "Mega Backdoor" Roth

This strategy is for people whose work 401(k) plans have some special features. It's like finding a secret tunnel that lets you move a lot more money into your Roth account. Here's the gist:

- You make extra contributions to your 401(k) beyond the usual limit.

- Then, you immediately move that money into a Roth IRA.

- If you can use this strategy, you might be able to put up to $58,000 per year into your Roth accounts.

3. Cash Balance Plans for Business Owners

If you own a business, you've got another powerful option in your playbook. It's called a cash balance plan, and you can use it alongside your 401(k). This plan is like strapping a rocket to your retirement savings and lighting the fuse. Depending on your age and income, you might be able to set aside $300,000 or more per year, and it's tax-deductible.

Unleashing the Power of Self-Directed IRAs: A Deep Dive

Now that we've covered the basics let's venture into more advanced territory. One of the most powerful yet often overlooked strategies for high-income earners is using self-directed IRAs for alternative investments. This approach can potentially supercharge your returns while maintaining the tax advantages of traditional retirement accounts.

What is a Self-Directed IRA?

A self-directed IRA is a type of Individual Retirement Account that allows you to invest in a much wider range of assets than traditional IRAs. While most IRAs limit you to stocks, bonds, and mutual funds, a self-directed IRA opens up a world of alternative investments.

Are you with me so far? Good, because here's where it gets exciting. You can invest in:

- Real estate
- Private company stock
- Precious metals

72

- Cryptocurrency

- Tax liens

- Private equity deals

- And much more

The key here is to have unprecedented control over your retirement funds, and the best way to achieve that is for you, not a custodian, to direct the investments.

How It Works: A Step-by-Step Guide

1. **Establish the Self-Directed IRA:** You'll need to work with a custodian who allows self-directed investments. Not all do, so choose carefully.

2. **Fund the Account:** You can fund your self-directed IRA through annual contributions, transfers from other IRAs, or rollovers from employer-sponsored plans like 401(k)s.

3. **Identify Investments:** Research and select alternative investments that align with your goals and risk tolerance.

4. **Direct the Custodian:** Instruct your custodian to make the investments on behalf of your IRA.

5. **Manage and Monitor:** Keep track of your investments and ensure compliance with IRS rules.

The Power of Alternative Investments: A Case Study

Let me tell you about Tom, a successful entrepreneur in his 40s. Tom had accumulated $500,000 in his traditional IRA, which was invested in a mix of stocks and bonds, yielding about 7% annually. Not bad, but Tom believed he could do better.

We helped Tom set up a self-directed IRA and use it to invest in a promising real estate development project. Here's how it played out:

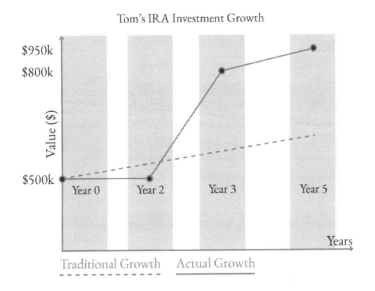

The best part? All of this growth occurred tax-deferred within the IRA. When Tom eventually takes distributions in retirement, he'll potentially have hundreds of thousands more to withdraw. I've seen this play out with my own clients time and time again. It's like watching a rookie become an all-star right before your eyes.

Navigating the Pitfalls: What to Watch Out For

Now, I'm not gonna sugarcoat it for you. While self-directed IRAs offer enormous potential, they also come with unique challenges. The IRS has more rules than J.Lo has wedding rings. Here's what you need to watch out for:

- **Prohibited Transactions:** The IRS has strict rules about who you can transact with using your IRA funds. Transactions with yourself, your spouse, your children, or their spouses are all prohibited. Violating these rules can disqualify your entire IRA.

- **Unrelated Business Income Tax (UBIT):** Certain investments, particularly those involving leverage or active businesses, may trigger UBIT, potentially reducing your returns.

- **Valuation Challenges:** Alternative assets can be difficult to value, complicating required minimum distributions (RMDs) when you reach age 72.

- **Fraud Risk:** The world of alternative investments can attract fraudsters. Thorough due diligence is crucial.

- **Lack of Liquidity:** Many alternative investments are illiquid, which can be problematic if you need to take distributions.

Advanced Strategies for the Savvy Investor

For those of you ready to take your self-directed IRA to the next level, consider these advanced tactics:

- **Checkbook Control:** By setting up an LLC owned by your IRA, you can gain checkbook control over your IRA funds, allowing for quicker, more flexible investing.

- **Roth Conversion Ladder:** Strategically convert portions of your traditional self-directed IRA to a Roth IRA over time, potentially minimizing taxes and maximizing long-term, tax-free growth.

- **Partnering IRAs:** If a deal is too big for your IRA alone, you can partner with other IRAs or even non-IRA funds to make larger investments.

- **Option Strategies:** Use your self-directed IRA to write options on real estate or other alternative assets, generating income while maintaining your core investments.

Striking it Rich on Black Gold

Now, let me tell you about my client, Jacques. This guy came to me with a traditional SEP IRA worth about

$100K. He had a hunch about the oil and gas industry but didn't know how to play it smart. That's where I came in.

We invested Jacques' $100K from his traditional SEP IRA into an oil and gas fund with a well-known company. Now, here's where it gets good. After making the investment, we converted his traditional SEP IRA into a Roth IRA. You know what that means? When the fund starts making distributions back into the account, those distributions and growth are tax-free inside the account and when Jacques withdraws them. Talk about a Texas tea party!

Now, I know what you're thinking. "Eric, won't that conversion trigger a big tax bill?" Well, here's the kicker. We did the conversion when the account balance was much lower, minimizing the tax hit from the conversion. It's all about timing, folks.

Fast-forward a year, and Jacques is about to receive the largest distribution that the fund has ever given out. And it's all tax-free. But wait, there's more. Per the fund's projections, Jacques is estimated to make 3X his investment in the next 5-10 years.

With this tax strategy, Jacques is feeling as giddy as the Beverly Hillbillies who struck oil. But instead of stumbling onto black gold, he created his own gusher through smart tax planning. He's living large like Jed Clampett but with a much better accountant. (That's me, in case you were wondering.)

Eric's Pro Tip:

"Don't underestimate the power of self-directed IRAs. Think beyond stocks and bonds when it comes to your retirement accounts!"

Bringing It All Together

Supercharging your retirement accounts involves more than just maxing out your contributions. It's about leveraging these tax-advantaged vehicles to their fullest potential through self-directed investing, strategic Roth conversions, and even funding business growth.

As with all advanced tax strategies, working with a knowledgeable professional is crucial to navigating complex rules and customizing a plan aligned with your financial goals. That's where I come in. I've seen these strategies work wonders for my clients, and I can help you navigate this complex terrain.

Your retirement accounts are powerful tools for building and protecting wealth. Used wisely, they can significantly accelerate your path to financial freedom. In the next chapter, we'll explore strategies for protecting your hard-earned wealth through smart estate planning.

Chapter 6

Protecting Your Legacy with Smart Estate Planning

You've spent years grinding away, building a fortune that would make your younger self's jaw drop. But here's the kicker - all that hard work could vanish faster than free donuts in the break room. And no, I'm not talking about a stock market crash or a bad investment gone south. I'm talking about what happens when successful people overlook one crucial piece of the wealth management puzzle: estate planning.

This reality hits many people who've made it big, and often, it's too late to do anything about it. But here's the good news - it doesn't have to be your story.

Estate planning is about securing life—the lives of those you care about and the legacy you want to leave behind. It's about making sure that all that wealth you've worked your tail off to build keeps making a positive impact long after you're gone.

In this chapter, we're gonna pull back the curtain on smart estate planning. We'll dive into how savvy entrepreneurs and high-rollers are using cutting-edge strategies to:

1. Slash their estate tax bill by millions.

2. Make sure their wealth empowers their kids instead of turning them into trust fund babies.

3. Support causes they're passionate about while scoring some sweet tax benefits.

4. Create a legacy that'll keep on giving long after they're gone.

From Tax Shock to Legacy Builder

Let me tell you about James, a client of mine who built a tech company from the ground up. At 55, he sold his business for $50 million and was ready to kick back and enjoy retirement. But as the champagne buzz wore off, a new worry set in. James had two kids in college and a newborn grandkid. He wanted to make sure his family would be taken care of, but when he found out how much of his hard-earned cash could end up in Uncle Sam's pocket, he nearly fell out of his ergonomic chair.

I've seen this scenario play out more times than I've

had hot dinners. Over the next few months, James and I rolled up our sleeves and got to work. We set up a bunch of trusts, cooked up a strategic gifting plan, and even used life insurance in a way that would make most people's heads spin faster than a basketball on Kyrie Irving's finger.

By the time we were done, we'd potentially saved James's family tens of millions in estate taxes. But here's what got me: I saw James change as we went through this process. The worry lines on his forehead started to smooth out. He began talking more about his hopes for his grandkids' future and less about his fears of estate taxes. He even started planning a scholarship fund at his alma mater—something he'd never thought he could afford before.

That's the real power of estate planning, folks. It's not just about keeping the taxman's hands out of your pockets - it's about maximizing the impact of your wealth, both for your family and for the causes you care about.

Now, let's break down some key estate planning concepts and strategies to help you achieve similar results.

Understanding Estate Taxes

Think of estate taxes like that surprise villain in a Marvel movie - you know it's coming, but you're never quite sure when or how hard it'll hit. As of 2021, Uncle Sam won't touch your estate unless it's worth more than $11.7 million (or $23.4 million for married couples). Sounds like a lot, right? But here's the thing - this generous exemption is set to drop dramatically in 2025, possibly down to around $6 million per person.

That's why it's crucial to start planning now, even if you're not quite in the multi-millionaire club yet. Even if you're under these thresholds, there are still plenty of reasons to get your estate planning game on point:

1. **State estate taxes:** Some states are grabbier than toddlers in toy stores and have much lower exemptions.

2. **Future growth:** Your estate might balloon past the exemption when you check out.

3. **Changing laws:** Tax laws are about as stable as a house of cards in a windstorm.

4. **Beyond taxes:** Estate planning isn't just about dodging taxes—it's about controlling who gets what and keeping your affairs on the low.

The Power of Trusts

Now, let's talk about the Swiss Army knife of estate planning: trusts. In simple terms, a trust is like a magic box where you put your assets, and a trustee (who could be you or someone else) manages them for your chosen beneficiaries.

There are more types of trusts than flavors at an ice cream shop, and trust me, some of them are just as complicated as trying to pronounce "Phish Food" with your mouth full. But here are a few popular ones:

1. **Revocable Living Trusts**: Think of these as your assets' VIP pass to skip the probate line.

2. **Irrevocable Life Insurance Trusts (ILITs)**: These keep your life insurance payout from becoming a tax bomb for your heirs.

3. **Grantor Retained Annuity Trusts (GRATs)**: Perfect for passing on assets you expect to skyrocket in value without gifting away the farm.

4. **Charitable Remainder Trusts (CRTs)**: These are for when you want to support a cause and get a tax break—talk about having your cake and eating it, too!

Strategic Gifting

Picture your taxable estate as an overinflated balloon. Strategic gifting is like slowly and deliberately releasing air from that balloon, gradually reducing its size over time. This approach allows you to transfer significant wealth to your beneficiaries while keeping the IRS off your back.

As of 2021, the IRS allows you to give away up to $15,000 per person per year without triggering gift tax consequences. This is known as the annual gift tax exclusion. It's a powerful tool that savvy estate planners use to their advantage. Here's how it works:

- You can give $15,000 to as many individuals as you like each year.

- This means $15,000 to each of your kids, each grandkid, and yes, even to your neighbor If you're feeling particularly generous!

- This amount doubles to $30,000 per recipient per year for married couples.

The beauty of a systematic gifting strategy is its cumulative effect. Over time, you can transfer a substantial portion of your estate to your beneficiaries, all while flying under the IRS radar. Let's crunch some numbers:

Suppose you have three kids and six grandkids. You and your spouse could potentially transfer $270,000 per year to your family members without any gift tax implications ($30,000 x 9 recipients). Over a decade, that amounts to $2.7 million moved out of your taxable estate.

Giver	Recipient	Annual Gift	Recipients	Total Annual Gifts	10-Year Total
You	Kids	$15,000	3	$45,000	$450,000
Spouse	Kids	$15,000	3	$45,000	$450,000
You	Grandkids	$15,000	6	$90,000	$900,000
Spouse	Grandkids	$15,000	6	$90,000	$900,000
Total		$30,000	9	$270,000	$2,700,000

This method creates a steady, controlled flow of wealth to your loved ones during your lifetime. It's like a well-executed play in basketball - you're passing the ball (your wealth) strategically to your teammates (your beneficiaries) while keeping the defense (the IRS) on their toes.

Family Limited Partnerships (FLPs) and Family Limited Liability Companies (FLLCs)

Think of these as your family's own private bank or investment firm. They're special business structures that let you manage and transfer wealth within the family. Here's what they can do for you:

1. Keep control in the family, usually with the older generation calling the shots.

2. Potentially slash the value of your assets in the

taxman's eyes.

3. Protect your assets from creditors like a financial fortress.

4. Make it easier to gift chunks of the family wealth over time.

Charitable Giving Strategies

For those of you with a philanthropic itch, there are ways to scratch it that'll make both your heart and your wallet happy. Here are a few options:

Charitable Lead Trusts (CLTs): Let a charity "borrow" your money for a while before it goes to your heirs.

Private Foundations: Start your own mini-charity and play Bill Gates for a day.

Donor-Advised Funds: Think of these as charitable savings accounts - you get the tax break now but can dish out the dough to charities later.

Last but not least, there's life insurance. It's not just for replacing your income anymore. When used right, it can be an ace up your sleeve in your estate planning game, providing tax-free cash to pay estate taxes or make sure all your kids get an equal slice of the pie.

Eric's Pro Tip:

"Estate planning isn't just for the ultra-wealthy. It's not just about what you leave behind but how you leave it. So let's get to work and make your legacy something to really brag about!"

Bringing It All Together

Let's pump the brakes for a second and look at the big picture. We've covered a lot of ground here, from trusts to gifting strategies, but what does it all really mean for you?

Estate planning is about you calling the shots on what happens to your hard-earned wealth. It's about making sure your kids, grandkids, or maybe that animal shelter you love, get the support you want to give them.

Think about it this way - you've spent your life building your wealth. Don't you want to have a say in what happens to it after you're gone? That's what all these strategies are there for. They're tools in your toolbox to shape your legacy.

Now, I get it. Reading all of this at once can make your head spin faster than a roulette wheel. Trusts, tax laws, gifting limits - it's a lot to take in. But here's a secret: you don't have to figure it all out on your own. That's what pros like me are for. The most important thing is to start thinking about what you want your legacy to be.

- What matters most to you?

- Who or what do you want to support?

Once you've figured that out, the rest is just details. It's game time. Are you ready to level up your legacy game? You've just gotten a crash course in estate planning, and I hope it's sparked some ideas about how you can protect your wealth and shape your legacy. But here's the thing - while knowing the strategies is great, implementing them is a whole different ball game.

You didn't build your wealth by going it alone. You had advisors, mentors, and partners along the way. Tackling your estate plan should be no different. If you're ready to take the next step and turn these ideas into a concrete plan tailored to your unique situation, it might be time to reach out to a professional who can help you navigate these waters.

Are you ready to be the MVP of your family's financial future? In the pages ahead, I'll share how you can get in touch if you want to explore these strategies further and start building your legacy. Because at the end of the day, it's not just about protecting your wealth - it's about creating a lasting impact that goes beyond your lifetime.

PART 3

THE PATH FORWARD

Chapter 7

Your Next Steps
Toward Financial Freedom

Congratulations! You've made it to the end of this playbook, and you're now equipped with knowledge that puts you ahead of the game when it comes to tax strategy. But let's keep it real - knowledge without action is like a high-performance sports car without gas. Impressive to look at, but it's not going anywhere. So, what's next? Let's map out your route to financial freedom.

The Power of Your Next Move

Before we dive into the game plan, I want you to take a moment to envision where you could be with your finances in one year, five years, or even a decade from now if you implement the strategies we've discussed. Picture the peace of mind that comes with knowing you're not overpaying taxes, that your wealth is growing efficiently, and that you're on the fast track to true financial freedom.

Every day you wait to take action is potentially costing you money. These strategies don't implement themselves, and the sooner you act, the more you stand to benefit. Let's turn that vision into reality.

Your 3-Step Action Plan

1. Set Clear Financial Goals

Tax strategy isn't just about paying less – it's about aligning your finances with your life goals. Take some time to define what you want to achieve:

- Short-term goals (1-3 years)

- Medium-term goals (3-10 years)

- Long-term goals (10+ years)

These might include business growth targets, personal milestones (like buying that vacation home you've been eyeing), or legacy plans for your wealth.

2. Identify Your Top 3 Tax-Saving Opportunities

Based on what you've learned in this book, which strategies seem most applicable to your situation? Maybe it's:

- Restructuring your business for better tax

efficiency

- Maximizing your retirement contributions
- Exploring real estate investments for tax benefits
- Implementing a charitable giving strategy

Choose the top three that you think could have the biggest impact on your tax situation.

3. Schedule Your Tax Strategy Session

This is where the rubber meets the road. It's time to sit down with a tax strategist who can help you implement these ideas in a way that's tailored to your specific situation.

The Complimentary Strategy Session

I'm so confident in the value I can provide that I'm offering readers of this book a complimentary, no-obligation 15-minute introductory call. This isn't a full-blown strategy session - think of it more as a chance for us to get to know each other and see if we're a good fit.

During this 15-minute call, we'll:

- Get a high-level overview of your current financial situation
- Discuss your main financial goals and concerns
- Explore how the strategies in this book might

apply to your circumstances

• Determine if a more in-depth strategy session would be beneficial for you

Remember, this introductory call is complimentary and carries no obligation. It's my way of showing you the value I can bring to your financial life.

How to Schedule Your 15-Minute Intro Call:

1. Visit: https://calendly.com/greattaxescape to schedule your 15-minute introductory call.

2. Come to our call prepared with your top financial questions and goals. This is your opportunity to get a taste of how we could work together to optimize your tax strategy.

Don't let another tax season slip by without taking control of your financial future. The wealthy didn't get where they are by leaving things to chance, and neither should you. Take this small step today, and let's explore how we can transform your tax burden into a wealth-building opportunity.

The Eric Pierre Difference: Working with a Flat Fee CPA

Let me break down why working with a flat fee CPA like myself can be a game-changer for your financial strategy:

1. Transparency: You'll know exactly what you're

paying for upfront. No surprises, no hidden fees.

2. **Aligned Interests:** Our goal is to maximize your tax savings, not our billable hours.

3. **Peace of Mind:** You won't have to worry about the meter running every time you need advice or have a question.

4. **Predictable Costs:** The fee only changes if there's work outside of our agreement. Otherwise, you're locked in.

5. **Clear Expectations:** With a flat fee structure, there are no misunderstandings about the scope of work or costs involved.

This approach allows us to focus on what really matters: optimizing your tax strategy and building your wealth.

Eric's Pro Tip:

"Success leaves clues. When I was building my practice, I studied the habits of high achievers. One common thread? They all had a strong team of advisors. Are you ready to build yours?"

Final Thoughts: Your Journey to Financial Freedom Starts Now

As we wrap up this book, I want to leave you with one final thought: you have the power to take control of your financial future. The strategies we've discussed aren't just theoretical concepts – they're practical tools that can dramatically impact your wealth-building journey.

Every day, I witness the transformative effect of smart tax planning on my clients' lives. I've seen entrepreneurs reinvest tax savings to exponentially grow their businesses. I've watched executives use these strategies to retire years earlier than they thought possible. I've helped families create legacies that will benefit generations to come.

You've already taken the first step by reading this book. Now, I invite you to take the next step. Schedule your introductory call. Put these ideas into action. Start your journey towards true financial freedom.

Remember, in the world of taxes and wealth-building, knowledge isn't just power – it's profit. You now have the knowledge. Are you ready to turn it into prosperity?

I look forward to being your guide on this exciting journey. Here's to your financial success!

Resources and Social Media

Connect with me on social media
for regular insights and updates:

Instagram
https://www.instagram.com/pierreaccounting/

Facebook
https://www.facebook.com/pierreaccounting/

Twitter
https://twitter.com/PierreCPA

Podcast: Sports Gumbo

Sports Gumbo is where I blend my passion for sports with my financial and business side. As a CPA, tax expert, business leader, former professional athlete, philanthropist, and sports enthusiast, I bring a unique perspective to the table.

Join me, my co-host Drew Lasker, and a variety of guests as we explore a rich mix of topics at the intersection of sports, business, and current events. It's a different flavor from what we've discussed in this book. Still, you might be surprised at how often financial wisdom pops up in our conversations.

If you're curious, you can find Sports Gumbo on Spotify. Direct your Phone's camera to the QR link below to listen to it now:

About the Author

Eric Pierre is the CPA who's rewriting the rules of the CPA game. With 17 years in the trenches of accounting, tax, and finance, Eric's not your average number-cruncher. He's the mastermind behind Pierre Accounting, the go-to resource for high-net-worth individuals looking to keep more of their hard-earned cash out of Uncle Sam's pocket.

Eric didn't just wake up one day and decide to be a tax wizard. He cut his teeth in the corporate world, running with the big dogs at Fortune 500 giants like Deloitte

& Touche and Abbott Laboratories. This brother crunched numbers from Asia to Africa, Europe to the Caribbean. Energy, pharma, you name it - he's seen it all.

But the corporate world was like a pair of dress shoes a size too small for Eric. They looked good, but man, did they pinch. So, in 2015, he laced up his own kicks and founded Pierre Accounting. His mission? Helping high-income earners and successful business owners keep more of their hard-earned millions through sophisticated, fully vetted, and 100% legal tax strategies.

Education? Eric's got that on lock. Master's degree and bachelor's degree, both with honors, from Stephen F. Austin State University. CPA licenses in Texas and California? Check and check. But here's the kicker - he's a second-generation CPA. It's in his DNA, folks.

Eric's not just any CPA. He runs with an elite crew of tax pros. They're like the Avengers of the accounting world, always on top of the latest tax law changes and planning techniques. For Eric, it's not about playing the game; it's about changing it.

When he's not saving clients millions, you can catch Eric courtside. Basketball is his jam, and he even co-hosts a podcast mixing sports and finance. Talk about a power play.

But it's not all about the Benjamins for Eric. He's big on giving back. Prison reform and educational scholarships

- if it's about lifting people up, he's all in.

And yeah, Eric's got dreams. Owning an NBA team is on his vision board. Because why dream small when you can dream big?

He splits his time between offices in Austin, San Diego, and Los Angeles, bringing his expertise to a diverse clientele across the country. He's turning tax bills into investment opportunities and making money work as hard as his clients do.

In the world of finance, Eric's not just playing chess while others play checkers. He's mastering every piece on the board, always a few moves ahead. While some CPAs stick to the basic rules, Eric strategizes at a grandmaster level, using every legal move in the playbook to help his clients win the game of wealth preservation.

Made in the USA
Columbia, SC
17 October 2024

f74a8719-5218-4eaf-9a34-8a23a113a8a1R02